NETWORK

The Right People... In the Right Places... For the Right Reasons

CONSULTANT'S GUIDE

Bruce Bugbee · Don Cousins · Bill Hybels

ZondervanPublishingHouse
Grand Rapids, Michigan
A Division of HarperCollinsPublishers

Network: Consultant's Guide
Copyright © 1994 by Willow Creek Community Church

Requests for information should be addressed to:
Zondervan Publishing House
Grand Rapids, Michigan 49530

Edited by Jack Kuhatschek and Rachel Boers
Cover design by John M. Lucas
Interior design by Paetzold Design

ISBN 0-310-41221-8

96 / 97 / 98 / CH / 9 / 8 / 7 / 6 / 5 / 4

NETWORK

...

TO

VALERIE

For the many years
she has so faithfully
served me and our four children:
Brittany, Brianne, Bronwyn, and Todd.

CONTENTS

I consider the development of the Network materials to be one of the most significant breakthroughs in the history of Willow Creek Community Church.

We discovered years ago that believers flourish in their service to Christ when they are serving in the area of their giftedness and in conjunction with their God-given uniqueness. The Network materials grew out of our desire to help believers discover their spiritual gifts, and then determine where to use them in our church body.

The results of Network have been astounding. Imagine having fresh servants entering the work force of the church every year, confident of their giftedness and eager to invest them in service for God's glory.

It is happening!

May God bless you as you learn and grow through these tremendous materials.

Bill Hybels
Senior Pastor
Willow Creek Community Church

It has been said that "there is nothing new under the sun" (Ecclesiastes 1:9). These Network materials bear witness to that timeless truth.

I have attempted to put together a simple and easy-to-walk-through process for believers who desire to serve in the local church. In doing so I have utilized the insights of many authors, teachers, leaders, and servants. This material has been adapted, edited, and written to present a comprehensive and consistent approach for those who desire to do ministry. But it could not have been done without the input and assistance of many people.

Peter Wagner's vision inspired me to see Spiritual Gifts understood, discovered, and used in ministry. His excellent seminar materials laid a foundation for my thinking.

Tim Cranston provided excellent leadership in the training of many consultants and in the development of these training materials.

Mary Lou Kahn's sensitivity and commitment to highly qualified consultants has contributed to many of the insights reflected in this guide.

Special thanks to Tom Threlkeld, Cher Pociask, Tom Moder, Ken Bado, Dave Krieger, and a host of other caring consultants who have been instrumental in sending thousands of motivated servants into meaningful places of service.

Wendy Guthrie has made comprehensive contributions to the interactive learning that is now a part of Network. Her commitment to quality communication and biblical truth will benefit each participant. She has been a gracious project manager in the development of this new format.

John Nixdorf brought training expertise and perspective to the rewriting process. His patient and persistent spirit made an otherwise tedious task fun and meaningful.

Jim Mellado served as the catalyst to move the existing materials into this new international phase. He had started a Network Ministry and shares the passion and vision for what God is doing through the Network process.

I appreciate the Willow Creek Association[SM] for its support and assistance in making these materials available to even greater numbers of believers. Their conferences have provided many exciting opportunities to present Network to Christian leaders around the world.

And a special thanks to those who have participated in Network at Willow Creek Community Church. Your feedback and support have freed me to be more faithful and diligent in my own service to the body of Christ.

To all these people, and the many others who are so faithfully using their gifts, thank you. Together, we can serve yet a greater body of believers who want their lives to count for Christ and impact the world for which he died.

Bruce Bugbee
President
Network Ministries International

I. INTRODUCTION

BEFORE THE CONSULTANT TRAINING

Congratulations on your decision to participate in Network Consultant Training. As a Network Consultant, you will play a major role both in our church's Network ministry and in the lives of the people you consult.

To gain the most from the Network Consultant Training, please do the following as pre-class preparation:

- ❑ Read this Consultant's Guide
- ❑ Highlight or note any areas where you have questions
- ❑ Review the role-play situation provided in the Appendix of this guide
- ❑ Assemble your Network participant materials, make sure you have completed your *Servant Profile* and *Personal Resources Survey*
- ❑ Bring these materials with you to the Network Consultant Training program

CONSULTANT TRAINING PROGRAM

Objective

To equip you to conduct a personal, one-on-one session with a volunteer in order to help that person find a meaningful ministry for service.

Consultant Training Process

The following is a suggested training path for becoming a Network consultant:

1. Attend the Network Seminar
2. Be consulted
3. Observe two consultations *
4. Study Ministry Position Descriptions
5. Review your church's structure of ministry and statement of faith
6. Training Day (Consultant's Guide)
7. Observe two consultations *
8. Join a consulting team with leader
9. Submit hours you are available to consult
10. BEGIN consulting

> * If you are in the *first* group of consultants in your church's Network ministry, you will not have the opportunity to observe consultations.

In this session, we will cover
- Theory and Procedures of successful Network consulting
- Role-play and practice, where we will apply the theory and procedures in "live" situations.

Materials

Your consultant materials consist of:
- This guide
- Network Vision and Consultant Training Video
- Ministry Position Descriptions

Other Resources to consider:
- Ministry leaders/staff
- Consultant Coordinator
- On-going skill training
- Other consultants

NETWORK'S GOAL

To help believers be fruitful and fulfilled in a meaningful place of service.

A believer will achieve that Goal by making his or her unique contribution to the body of Christ with his or her Passion, Spiritual Gifts, and Personal Style.

WHAT DOES THIS MEAN TO THE INDIVIDUAL?

Unique Contribution

The expression of who God made each individual to be in the way he or she performs a serving function.

Passion

Serving in a ministry for which he or she has enthusiasm and emotional energy.

Spiritual Gifts

Performing functions which use his or her particular giftedness.

Personal Style

Functioning relationally in a role that energizes the volunteer, rather than drains him or her emotionally.

Fruitful

Realizing positive results.

Fulfilled

Enhancing his or her esteem and sense of personal satisfaction by glorifying God and edifying others.

Meaningful

Sense of "making a difference."

Do Whatever It Takes To Serve Those Who Are Seeking To Serve.

CONSULTANT'S ROLES AND RESPONSIBILITIES

Consultants fulfill three roles:

1. Interpreter of the *Servant Profile*
   - Clarify and confirm volunteer *Servant Profile* conclusions (Passion, Spiritual Gifts, and Personal Style)
   - Affirm volunteer direction for possible areas of service
   - Identify volunteer development levels

2. Ambassador for the staff
   - Communicate different ministry goals and roles to the volunteer
   - Explain church philosophy to the volunteer
   - Agree with volunteer on his or her level of ministry responsibility at this time

3. Advocate for the volunteer
   - Research unanswered questions for the volunteer
   - Explore unique ministry possibilities with the volunteer and/or staff

Consultants are not responsible for:
   - Being a professional counselor
   - Fixing, healing, or saving
   - Filling placement quotas

Consultants are responsible for:
   - Faithfully participating in on-going training and development opportunities provided for consultants
   - Using initiative and keeping well-informed

Consultant's Goals:
   - Serve the volunteer personally
   - Be a grand encourager
   - Be a servant who honors God in word and deed

Note: Each person is different. Attempting to do a consultation with more than one person at a time does not allow you to provide the individualized attention that is the goal of Network's consultation. Sometimes one person can hinder the freedom of the other.

PREPARING FOR THE CONSULTATION

Setup

1. Call and confirm appointment time and location with volunteer two days in advance of the consultation. Remind the volunteer to bring his or her Network Participant Guide and that the consultation will be approximately one hour long.

2. Arrive at least twenty minutes early, review the volunteer's *Personal Resources Survey* (PRS). A copy of the PRS is provided in the Appendix of this guide.

Review *Personal Resources Survey*

Review and reflect on the volunteer's *Personal Resources Survey*. Pray for wisdom and for the volunteer.

Sample Consultation Outline

Think about each step of the consultation process and plan your time with the volunteer.

A sample consultation outline is provided below and in the Appendix of this guide.

1. Welcome
    a) Set the mood
    b) Prayer
    c) Paperwork
2. Determine the Volunteer's Motivation for Serving
3. Interpreting the *Servant Profile* and PRS Form
    a) Interpreting the *Servant Profile*
        (1) Passion
        (2) Spiritual Gifts
        (3) Personal Style
        (4) *Servant Profile* Summary

       b) Interpret Remaining Areas of the PRS Form
          (1) Talents, Abilities, Acquired Skills
          (2) Spiritual Maturity
          (3) Availability
          (4) Additional Items
4. Determine An Appropriate Ministry "M" Category
5. Identify Three Possible Ministries
6. Wrap up/Closure
       a) Complete The Next Step Form
       b) Affirm and Encourage
       c) Close in Prayer

THE CONSULTATION

WELCOME

Set the mood

Make the volunteer feel at home, take the initiative in breaking the ice and putting the volunteer at ease. Listed below are some possible greetings:

- How was your day today?
- I've been looking forward to meeting with you
- I'm a volunteer too
- I've been praying about our time together

Prayer

Begin the consultation by seeking the Lord's wisdom and peace and acknowledging his presence.

Paperwork

If the volunteer did not turn in the *Personal Resources Survey* form prior to the consultation, ask for it at this time.

DETERMINE THE VOLUNTEER'S MOTIVATION FOR SERVING

Begin your dialogue with the volunteer by asking opening questions that will help you understand the volunteer's motivation and expectations. Note: throughout the consultation, use as many open-ended questions as possible to allow the volunteer to express him/herself.

Examples:

- How did you like the Network Sessions?
- Why did you attend Network at this time?
- Tell me how you came to our church?
- What has motivated you to serve at this time?
- What are you seeking from this consultation?
- What is the Holy Spirit leading you to do?

In asking these types of questions, you can begin to determine:

- Whether this person really wants to serve
- When he or she wants to serve
- How *you* can best serve the volunteer
- Whether the volunteer considers this his or her church home

INTERPRETING THE *SERVANT PROFILE* AND PRS FORM

Overview

The purpose of this step is to clarify the volunteer's level of understanding about his or her *Servant Profile* (Passion, Spiritual Gifts, Personal Style), talents, spiritual maturity, and availability.

The volunteer's *Servant Profile* and *Personal Resources Survey* (PRS) form are your guide for the dialogue portion of the consultation. During your dialogue with the volunteer, use your best listening skills. Let the volunteer reveal as much of him or herself as you can.

Use the *Servant Profile* and PRS form as a conversation guide. Begin asking questions designed to affirm, clarify, and confirm the volunteer's self-understanding of his or her results. Do not simply accept the answers given on the form as absolute conclusions, but rather as opportunities for dialogue and reflection.

As you discuss the *Servant Profile* and PRS form, you will begin to determine the levels of development and characteristics which establish the uniqueness of the volunteer.

Your assessment of his or her developmental level is based on your perception of how the volunteer might be viewed from the ministry leader's perspective relative to other volunteers.

A blank PRS form which includes the *Servant Profile* is provided in the Appendix of this guide.

Your awareness and discernment in the following subjective areas can be additional components in your overall assessment of a volunteer. You may want to make some special comments on the PRS form for the ministry leaders to note about these areas.

Attitude is important. Ministry leaders desire those who have an attitude of humility and a teachable spirit. Pride and an independent spirit are contrary to the purpose and goals for ministry.

Authenticity refers to the integrity in an individual's personal relationship with Jesus Christ and the natural ways that relationship is expressed to others. Does there seem to be consistency in his or her talk about Christ with his or her walk in the world?

Communication is important in ministries with a requirement for interpersonal skills. Is the person articulate? Be aware of eye contact, speech patterns, body language, listening skills, voice tone, expressed attitudes.

Self Esteem items include a sense of personal warmth, a healthy ego, and confidence.

INTERPRET THE *SERVANT PROFILE*

Passion

The purpose is to determine an appropriate level of development and emotional intensity of Passion.

Passion answers the "where" question

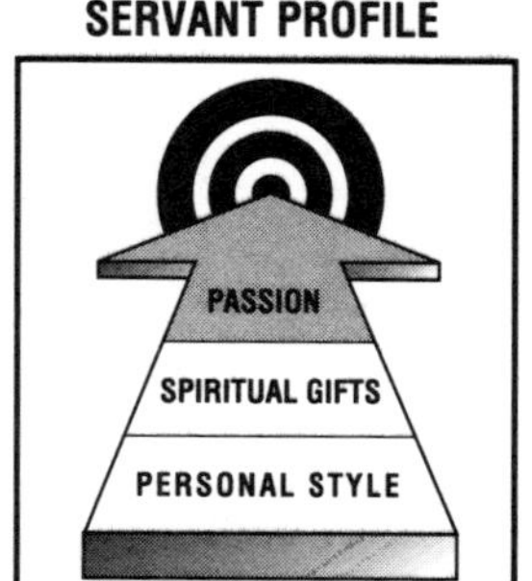

Passion may be the best indicator of where this person might have the highest energy and motivation to serve over the long haul.

Key Determiner: Emotional Intensity

The following examples of prompting questions may help to clarify the Passion statement and determine the volunteer's level of emotional intensity in that area:

When you wrote your Passion statement, what did you really mean?
- What ages of people?
- What circumstances?
- How do you think you might help?
- Where would you like to make a difference?
- What would you do, or change, if you could?

Developmental Levels Concerning Passion

Untested/Uncertain

The volunteer may express some emotional intensity for a Passion area but have little or no experience serving in that area.

Or the volunteer may have had some experience serving in an area and think that this might be his or her "Passion." The volunteer, however, exhibits very low emotional intensity, or excitement, as he or she talks about his or her experience. In this case you will want to probe for other possible Passion areas.

Moderate

Some emotional intensity with some limited experience.

Significant

The volunteer articulates excitement and enthusiasm for a Passion area and has served in this area in the past.

Proven/Affirmed

Considerable past experience in a ministry area. High emotion and commitment to that area. This person *really* cares about a particular ministry area. There may be no other ministry the volunteer would want to consider.

NOTE: If there is lack of clarity concerning the volunteer's Passion, then review the *Passion* Assessment for other possible themes or patterns. Remember, Passion can develop over time. It may start with only a mild interest level at first.

❑ On the PRS form, write in the volunteer's developmental level of Passion.

Spiritual Gifts

The purpose is to determine the volunteer's Spiritual Gift developmental level.

Spiritual Gifts answer the "what" question

The unique giftedness of the volunteer will indicate what the volunteer might do in a ministry which is consistent with his or her area of Passion.

Key Determiner: Past effectiveness

The following examples of prompting questions may help to determine the volunteer's current or past levels of effectiveness in using a Spiritual Gift:
   • Were you surprised by the Spiritual Gifts you
      discovered, or their order?
   • Why do you think this Spiritual Gift might be true
      for you?
   • How have you used this Spiritual Gift before in
      ministry?
   • Have you been affirmed by others when using this
      Spiritual Gift? How?
   • When have you felt effective in using this Spiritual Gift?

Be aware that for new believers and some others, determining "what" they should do in ministry will be based more on their natural talents or abilities than their spiritual giftedness. However, still attempt to lead with their Spiritual Gifts as much as you can.

Development Levels Concerning Spiritual Gifts

Untested/Uncertain

The volunteer has never before served in ministry. Spiritual gifts are new concepts to him or her.

Likely/Probable

The volunteer has some experience serving in some minor or limited capacities using the gift. Possibly the volunteer gives you the impression as being very consistent with a gift trait, for example: organizer (Administration), encourager (Encouragement), take charge/motivator (Leadership). This might indicate a higher than normal probability that the volunteer has that particular gift.

Affirmed/Developed

The volunteer has used the gift before in ministry and seems to have been affirmed by others in using the gift. He or she has had a significant level of effectiveness in using the gift.

Proven/Confirmed

The volunteer seems to have really developed his or her effectiveness in using the gift. Additionally, he or she is effective to a point where he or she has, or could, lead and develop this gift in others.

Caution: Some people are very mature and confident. This does not necessarily mean they have a particular Spiritual Gift. Don't confuse competence in one area with Spiritual Gift effectiveness.

NOTE: If there is lack of clarity concerning the volunteer's Spiritual Gifts, review the Spiritual Gifts assessments for other possible patterns. When discussing Spiritual Gifts, you may find it helpful to refer to the specific gift information found in the *Spiritual Gifts Reference Assessment* in the Network Participant Guide. Reexamining a gift with a volunteer may help clarify and confirm that person's understanding of whether a particular gift is true for him or her.

❏ On the PRS form, write in the volunteer's developmental level of Spiritual Gifts.

Personal Style

The purpose is to determine the serving context in which the volunteer would be most energized and organized.

Personal Style answers the "how" question

Understanding Personal Style is important in order to move volunteers toward those ministry positions which seem most natural for them. Servants serve better when their role expresses God-given preferences. How comfortable is the volunteer with his or her Personal Style?

Key Determiner: Flow of energy

The following questions may be helpful:
1. In what ways do you feel that the *Personal Style Assessment* reflects or doesn't reflect you?
2. Describe the ideal environment in which you would feel most energized and organized.
3. Can you give an example of a situation in which you feel unorganized?
4. Can you give an example of a situation in which you feel de-energized?

NOTE: If there is lack of clarity concerning the volunteer's Personal Style, then review the Personal Style Assessment. Remember developmental levels do not apply to Personal Style.

❑ On the PRS form, verify the box checked which reflects the volunteer's Personal Style.

Servant Profile Summary

Complete this sentence by reading it aloud to the volunteer and inserting his or her Passion, Spiritual Gifts, and Personal Style:

So, you see yourself as a
[*volunteer's Personal Style*] person that would like to
[*volunteer's Passion*] by
[*volunteer's Spiritual Gift*]?

Example: So you see yourself as a
task-oriented/structured person that would like to serve
the *homeless* by
giving/helping.

Do you feel fairly comfortable with that at this time?

INTERPRET REMAINING AREAS OF THE PRS FORM

Talents, Abilities, Acquired Skills

Here the purpose is to determine any talents, abilities, and/or acquired skills which could be used in conjunction with the volunteer's Spiritual Gifts.

Does this person have any talents or abilities in which he or she is competent and confident?

Examples: Nurse, social worker, piano tuner, photographer, computer programmer, carpenter, decorator, etc.

Important! Do not start with talents and abilities. People need to serve according to their Passion, Spiritual Gifts, and Personal Style *first*. There can be a tendency to look to a person's talents to see what they can do. But often, what someone has done in the past does not reflect their God-given Passion, Spiritual Gifts, and Personal Style.

Since our natural talents and abilities are also a part of our design, we do want to explore what ways (if any) they may complement our unique contribution in the ministry.

Talents can be an indicator of giftedness, but do not necessarily equate to Spiritual Gifts.

In Network a distinction is made between Spiritual Gifts and natural talents. While Spiritual Gifts are unique to the believer, talents are common to all. Both are God-given. Just as experiences and character traits may indicate a particular Spiritual Gift, so may talents. The affirmation of any Spiritual Gift must be consistent with glorifying God and edifying others.

Talents are not simply interests. Be sure what has been listed on the PRS form is something the volunteer has done before and has demonstrated a reasonable amount of competence.

Example questions:

- What are you doing that you do well?
- Do you have any special hobbies or pastimes?
- Have you had any specific training in some area?
- What skills have you especially worked hard to develop?

❏ On the PRS form, verify which talents, skills or abilities the volunteer could use in conjunction with his or her Spiritual Gifts.

Spiritual Maturity

Here the purpose is to determine the volunteer's level of Spiritual Maturity.

Key Determiner: Spiritual journey statement

The following examples of prompting questions may help the volunteer to describe his or her spiritual journey:
- Why did you circle the level you did on the *Servant Profile* form?
- How has your spiritual journey changed your life?
- Tell me about some aspect of your spiritual journey statement on the *Personal Resources Survey.*

Development Levels Concerning Spiritual Maturity

Following are the Network descriptions of Spiritual Maturity levels:

Seeker

You are gaining a better understanding of Christ and the Christian faith, but you have not yet personally trusted Jesus for the forgiveness of your sins. You are still investigating Christianity, still seeking truth.

New/Young Believer

You have recently become a Christian, and you are excited and enthused about your new walk with Jesus Christ, or you have been a Christian for some time, but you are just now learning what Jesus meant when He promised abundant life. In either case, you need to grow further in your understanding of the basics of the Christian faith and of what it means to walk daily in a personal relationship with Christ.

Stable/Growing Believer

You are confident of God's faithfulness and his ability to accomplish his will in your life. You are teachable and sensitive to the Spirit's leading. You exhibit the stability that comes from knowing Christ, regularly worshiping with his people, and actively pursuing a life of greater devotion.

Leading/Guiding Believer

You have demonstrated a consistent, mature walk with Christ. You are able to model faithfulness and inspire other believers. You can lead by example and guide others in a deeper understanding of what it means to walk personally with Jesus Christ.

NOTE: If there is lack of clarity concerning the volunteer's level of Spiritual Maturity, then have the volunteer describe in greater detail his or her spiritual walk.

❑ On the PRS form, verify the box checked which reflects the volunteer's level of Spiritual Maturity.

Availability

Here the purpose is to determine the volunteer's level of availability.

A volunteer may easily over- or under-estimate his or her time availability. It is important to have the volunteer consider issues such as:

- number in family
- commuting distance
- vocational time demands
- ages of children
- stage of life
- single/married

Do not hesitate to probe this area carefully. The volunteer may be reluctant or appear too busy to serve. Or their lifestyle may be presently too full to responsibly commit to doing more. If this is the case, discuss how their priorities are being reflected in their present choices. Ask them to consider what appropriate adjustments in their lifestyle may need to take place in order for them to reflect the priority of service in their life. What could they change in the next several weeks and months to be better able to make their unique contribution? You can best serve the volunteer and the ministry leaders by accurately considering the appropriate level of availability.

Example questions to explore availability:

- How might serving effect your present time commitments?
- Have you considered serving with a family member?
- Do you feel you could make a six-month or one-year commitment?

• Is there any pending development which might change your plans?

Developmental Levels Concerning Availability

Limited: One to two hours per week

Moderate: Two to four hours per week

Significant: Four or more hours per week

Not Sure: Not at this time

NOTE: If there is lack of clarity concerning the volunteer's level of availability, suggest a "limited" commitment (which would require 1 to 2 hours per week) or no commitment at this time. If it is the latter decision, suggest that the volunteer take the next few months to decide how to move toward service.

❏ On the PRS form, check the box which reflects the volunteer's availability to serve.

Additional Items

If appropriate discuss any remaining items on the PRS form (e.g., employment, education, church involvement) to gain further information for placement.

DETERMINE AN APPROPRIATE MINISTRY "M" CATEGORY

After completing the dialogue step, the consultant needs to come to an agreement with the volunteer about which overall ministry category best describes where the volunteer is at this time. Most people start at M1 or M2. Those who are already serving, and may be making a ministry change might be referred to as M3 positions.

Finding the right step to take is important. Use the chart below *as a guide*, so you and the volunteer can do a better job at placement.

	What is your current level of availability? (hours per week)			
What is your current level of spiritual maturity?	0-1	1-2	2-4	4+
Seeker	M1	M1	M1	M1
New/Young Believer	M1	M2	M2	M2
Stable/Growing Believer	M1	M2	M3	M3
Leading/Guiding Believer	M1	M2	M3	M4

See chart on the following page for a description of the "M" categories.

The Four Ministry Categories

Faithfulness Factor	Ministry Category	Category Descriptions
Start Here	M1 ➤	• Minimum availability required: Limited • Gifts/Passion are untested • Skills/Experience not required • Minimum maturity required: Seeker • Church membership not required
Start Here	M2 ➤	• Minimum availability required: Limited • General Passion/Spiritual Gifts/Personal Style fit • Some skills/experience helpful • Minimum maturity required: New/Young Believer • Church membership not required
Developed Ministry Effectiveness With Relational Credibility	M3 ➤	• Minimum availability required: Moderate • Specific Passion/Spiritual Gifts/Personal Style fit • Specific skills/experience required • Minimum maturity required: Stable/Growing believer • Church membership encouraged
Performing Major Ministry Responsibilities And Oversight	M4 ➤	• Minimum availability required: Significant • Proven Passion/Spiritual Gifts/Personal Style Affirmed • Proven skills/experience • Minimum maturity required: Leading/Guiding believer • Church membership required • May require significant people management skills

Note: The "M" category is a description of where the volunteer is presently, not necessarily where the volunteer will be in the future.

Suggested Consultant Script For Gaining Agreement On Ministry Categories

You will need to review these categories with the volunteer, then lead into one or more of the following questions:

- Based on everything we've talked about, which "M" category do you feel best describes you now?
- What category of serving seems most appropriate to you at this time?
- It seems to me that the ___________ category best describes you now. Does that make sense to you?

If there is lack of agreement, postpone the decision and meet again within several weeks to discuss.

After The Consultation

❏ Write in the volunteer's "M" category on the *Personal Resources Survey* form.

IDENTIFY THREE POSSIBLE MINISTRIES

First explore in detail those ministry possibilities the volunteer has listed on his or her *Personal Resources Survey*. Explain the ministries and specific positions in which the volunteer has indicated some interest. When the volunteer's desires have first been discussed, then make any other suggestions you have about where their Passion, Spiritual Gifts, and Personal Style could serve the body. Watch for his or her response. DO NOT PUSH the volunteer into any of these options. Any suggestions you might make need to be assessed and agreed on by the volunteer.

In selecting ministries, its best to identify ministries that most closely align with the volunteer's Passion. Remind the volunteer that moving from one position to another is expected, remember "Ted's Story" from the Network Discovery sessions. When specific ministries seem appropriate, you are ready to bring the consultation to a close.

If there is not agreement, or if you cannot affirm the direction the volunteer desires to go, then suggest that he or she spend some more time in prayer and reflection in light of the issues you have discussed. Agree to give the volunteer a call in seven to ten days.

❏ On the PRS form, list the ministries that you referred the volunteer to.

WRAP-UP/CLOSURE

Bring the consultation to closure:

1. Restate the top three ministries agreed upon.
2. List these three ministries and ministry contacts on the volunteer's Next Step form found in the Appendix.
3. Clearly emphasize the volunteer's responsibility to contact the ministry leaders to discuss possible involvement. Network refers the volunteer to potential areas of ministry, but it is the ministry leaders who will confirm, place, orient and train.
4. Encourage the volunteer. The volunteer is a significant member of the body of Christ. Praise the volunteer for taking his or her worship through service as seriously as he

or she has. Communicate your enthusiasm for his or her desire
to make a unique contribution to Christ and his church.

5. Close in Prayer. Affirm the Lord's hand in the volunteer's
life. Ask for the Lord's guidance and blessing on the
volunteer's life and ministry.

6. Give the Next Step form to the volunteer.

POST-CONSULTATION PAPERWORK

After the volunteer has left, make any special notes or comments in the "comments" section of the PRS form. Also, make copies of the volunteer's completed PRS form: one for your records, one for each of the three ministry leaders, and one for the Network files.

FOLLOW-UP

The purpose of follow-up is to encourage the volunteer.

The consultant's interpreter and ambassador roles are primarily fulfilled within the consultation. After the volunteer has completed the consultation, your advocate role becomes the priority. The goal of the advocate is to be sure that the volunteer who you consulted is responsibly recruited and assimilated in one of the ministries to which the volunteer was referred.

Guide for timing your follow-up:

First contact ➠ Two weeks after consultation
Second contact ➠ Four weeks after consultation
Third contact ➠ As needed

Follow-up after the consultation is to determine whether the volunteer made contact with the ministries.

If *yes*, then ask:

- Have you made a commitment to join this team?
- Will you be involved in a time of observation before commitment?
- When will you be trained?
- When do you start serving?
- What will you be doing when you start serving?

If *no*, encourage the volunteer to make contact with the
selected ministries, and inform him or her that you will be
back in touch within another two weeks.

If necessary, interact with ministry leaders and mediate any
issues that may have made the volunteer's placement difficult.
Use the *Network Consultant Follow-up Report,* in the
Appendix of this guide, to keep notes and dates of all follow-
up contacts.

CONSULTANT'S RESPONSIBILITY

1. Be at the church for the hours for which you have committed.
2. If you are unable to make your appointment because of an emergency or illness situation, call the church office immediately.

3. _______________________________________

4. _______________________________________

CANCELLATIONS

Your church needs to determine who should be contacted for cancellations.

SCHEDULING

Use one **master schedule**.

When a volunteer calls for an appointment, he or she is scheduled according to an available time slot on the master schedule. Do not assume that because one of your time slots was open a week beforehand that you are still unscheduled. A sample master schedule form is provided in the Appendix of this guide.

NO-SHOWS AND LATE ARRIVALS

If you have waited twenty minutes past the scheduled time of the appointment, you may consider it a "no-show."

HELPFUL THOUGHTS

Follow your gut — verbalize impressions and leading.

Deal with the problem — deal with issues in love, do not pass them on. Speak the truth in love.

Servanthood vs. Servility — is the volunteer's motivation for service authentic?

Delay a decision — it is OK to get back together in a week or two. Do not rush or push a decision. Suggest meeting again in a few weeks after a time of reflection and prayer.

Put your name on the line — can you find a reason for your recommendations?

Get your house in order — does the volunteer need to tie up loose ends or bring closure to present activities?

Proven faithfulness — Spiritual Gifts must be affirmed over time. Certain positions (for example leadership or teaching positions) need to have character and credibility affirmed.

Expect attacks — we are doing spiritual battle; non-serving Christians don't make a difference. Satan attacks serving Christians.

It's God's ministry — we are gifted to do the Lord's work, his way.

Remember — Without serving, people will never know how God can use him or her. Serving others who want to serve God is a double blessing.

KEEPING ON TRACK

If the conversation seems to be wandering away from the
purpose of the consultation, consider the following transitions
or bridging statements:

- This sounds like an expression of a possible______________
  Spiritual Gift.
- How does this experience relate to your _______________
  (Passion, Spiritual Gift, etc.).
- I sense your concern about this issue could be better
  addressed by speaking with _________________________
  (staff person or ministry leader).

There are times in the midst of a consultation when you can
best serve the volunteer by directing him or her to a ministry
leader that can better answer *the volunteer's* questions or con-
cerns. Make that referral or suggestion, and if appropriate,
keep moving through the consultation.

APPENDIX

PERSONAL RESOURCES SURVEY — 1

PERSONAL

Name _______________________ Network Session Month /Year ___/___

Address _________________________________ Apt# __________

City State Zip ____

Home Phone (___) ______________ Work Phone (___) ____________

Birth Date ________________ ❏ Male ❏ Female

FAMILY

Marital Status: ❏ Single   ❏ Married

Spouse's name: ________________________ Birthdate: ______________

Children names:

_______________________ ❏ M   ❏ F   Birthdate: ____________
_______________________ ❏ M   ❏ F   Birthdate: ____________
_______________________ ❏ M   ❏ F   Birthdate: ____________
_______________________ ❏ M   ❏ F   Birthdate: ____________
_______________________ ❏ M   ❏ F   Birthdate: ____________
_______________________ ❏ M   ❏ F   Birthdate: ____________

CHURCH

When did you start attending the church? Month/Year: ______/__________
Are you a member?   ❏ Yes   ❏ No
Small Groups: ❏ I am in one (Leader's name ______________)
                        ❏ I would like to be in one
                        ❏ I used to be in one (Leader's name ________)
                        ❏ Other: ______________________________

CURRENT MINISTRY INVOLVEMENT

Which ministries are you now involved in?   ❏ None
Ministry _______________ Leader _______________
Ministry _______________ Leader _______________
List other ministries or community groups outside the
church in which you are involved:
Ministry/Group _________________________________
Ministry/Group _________________________________

PAST MINISTRY INVOLVEMENT

Which ministries have you been involved in in the past?   ❏ None
Ministry _______________ Leader _______________
Ministry _______________ Leader _______________
List other ministries or community groups outside the church in which you
have been involved:
Ministry/Group _________________________________
Ministry/Group _________________________________

PERSONAL RESOURCES SURVEY — 2

SERVANT PROFILE AND CONSULTATION SUMMARY

**Complete Prior To
Your Consultation**

I have a **Passion** for:

1. _______________________

2. _______________________

My **Spiritual Gifts** are:

1. _______________________

2. _______________________

3. _______________________

**Shaded Area To Be Completed
By Consultant**

Passion

1. _______________________

2. _______________________

Spiritual Gifts

1. _______________________

2. _______________________

3. _______________________

My **Personal Style** is: ❏ People-Oriented/Structured   ❏ People-Oriented/Unstructured
❏ Task-Oriented/Structured   ❏ Task-Oriented/Unstructured

I would describe my **spiritual maturity** as:
❏ Seeker   ❏ New/young believer
❏ Stable/growing believer   ❏ Leading/guiding believer

I would describe my current **availability** as:
❏ Limited, 1-2 hrs   ❏ Moderate, 2-4 hrs
❏ Significant, 4+ hrs   ❏ Not sure

I would like to know more about the following ministries:

____

____

The following ministries were identified as
possible places of service: M Category: _______________

A. _______________   B. _______________   C. _______________

Consultant: _______________________   Phone: _______________

Comments: _______________________________________

____

PERSONAL RESOURCES SURVEY — 3

EMPLOYMENT

❑ I am employed   ❑ Self Employed   ❑ Unemployed

Name of Company ______________________________________

Title/Responsibilities__________________________________

Product or service ____________________________________

EDUCATION

❑ High School   ❑ Some College   ❑ Other__________

❑ College   ❑ Masters Degree

❑ Doctorate   ❑ Professional Degree

SPIRITUAL JOURNEY

How did you come to know Christ personally? How do you maintain your relationship?

____

____

____

____

____

____

____

____

____

____

____

____

____

____

____

____

____

____

PERSONAL RESOURCES SURVEY — 4

In addition to your *Servant Profile*, please go through each area, carefully marking the boxes which indicate talents or skills in which you have proven ability. In other words, indicate areas in which you have demonstrated a reasonable amount of confidence and competence. You are not making a commitment to serve in any area where you check a box, but we would like to have this information on file in case of special needs. Be honest and fair in your self-evaluation.

Professional Services

❑ Mental Health
❑ Social Work

❑ Financial
❑ Dental
❑ Medical

❑ Chiropractic
❑ Legal
❑ Accounting
❑ Bookkeeping
❑ Taxes
❑ Nursing
❑ Landscaping
❑ Carpet Cleaning
❑ Window Washing
❑ Engineer: ______
❑ Lifeguard
❑ Counseling
❑ Career Counseling
❑ Unemployment
❑ Day Care Director
❑ Law Enforcement
❑ Personnel Mgr.
❑ Public Relations
❑ Advertising
❑ Television: _____
❑ Radio
❑ Computer Prog.
❑ Paramedic/EMT
❑ Systems Analyst
❑ Journalist/Writer
❑ ______________

Art
❑ Layout
❑ Photography
❑ Graphics
❑ Multi-Media
❑ Typesetting
❑ Crafts
❑ Artist
❑ Banners
❑ Decorating
❑ ______________

Teaching or Assisting

❑ Preschool
❑ Elementary

❑ Junior High
❑ Senior High
❑ Single Adults (18-29)
❑ Single Adults (30+)
❑ Couples
❑ Men's Group
❑ Women's Group
❑ Tutoring
❑ Learning Disabled
❑ Researcher
❑ Aerobics
❑ Budget Counselor
❑ ______________

Mechanical
❑ Copier Repair
❑ Diesel Mechanic
❑ Auto Mechanic
❑ Small eng. Repair
❑ Mower Repair
❑ Machinist
❑

Office Skills
❑ Typing (40+ wpm)
❑ Word Processing
❑ Receptionist
❑ Office Manager
❑ Data Entry
❑ Filing
❑ Mail Room
❑ Library
❑ Transcription
❑ Shorthand
❑ ______________

Missions
❑ Missionary
❑ Evangelism
❑ ______________

Theatrical

❑ Actor/Actress
❑ Poet

❑ Dance
❑ Mime
❑ Puppets

❑ Clowning
❑ Audio Production
❑ Sound/Mixing
❑ Lighting
❑ Set Construction
❑ Set Design
❑ Stage Hand
❑ Script Writer
❑ ______________

Construction
❑ General Contractor
❑ Architect
❑ Carpenter: General
❑ Carpenter: Finish
❑ Carpenter: Cabinet
❑ Electrician
❑ Plumbing
❑ Heating
❑ Air Conditioning
❑ Painting
❑ Papering
❑ Masonry
❑ Roofing
❑ Telephones
❑ Drywall Finishing
❑ Concrete
❑ Carpet Installer
❑ Interior Design
❑ Drafting
❑ ______________

Working With

❑ Handicapped
❑ Hearing Impaired (Signing)
❑ Incarcerated
❑ Learning Disabilities
❑ Nursing Homes/ Shut-Ins
❑ Hospital Visitation
❑ Meals on Wheels
❑ Housing for Homeless
❑ ______________

General Help
❑ Cashier
❑ Child Care
❑ Customer Service
❑ Food Service
❑ Gardening
❑ Building Maintenance
❑ Grounds Maintenance
❑ Transportation
❑ Snow Removal
❑ Catering/Cooking
❑ Weddings
❑ Bookstore
❑ Tape Duplication
❑ Plant Care (Indoor)
❑ Sport Official
❑ Sports Instructor
❑ ______________

Musical
❑ Choir Director
❑ Choir
❑ Soloist
❑ Instrument
❑ Composer
❑ Arranger
❑ Piano Tuner
❑ ______________

Are there any other products, specific resources, skills, interests, talents, abilities, or unique opportunities (example: permitted access to specialized purchasing/discounts for the church) that you would like to offer to the church?

I understand that this information will be made available only to responsible and appropriate staff and ministry leaders at this church.

Signature: _______________________________ Date: _______________

1. Welcome
   a) Set the mood
   b) Prayer
   c) Paperwork
2. Determine the Volunteer's Motivation for Serving
3. Interpret the *Servant Profile* and PRS Form
   a) Interpret the *Servant Profile*
      (1) Passion
      (2) Spiritual Gifts
      (3) Personal Style
      (4) *Servant Profile* Summary
   b) Interpret Remaining Areas of the PRS
      (1) Talents, Abilities, Acquired Skills
      (2) Spiritual Maturity
      (3) Availability
      (4) Additional Items
4. Determine An Appropriate Ministry "M" Category
5. Identify Three Possible Ministries
6. Wrap up/Closure
   a) Complete The Next Step Form
   b) Affirm and Encourage
   c) Close in Prayer

NAME: _______________________________

The next step for me is to contact the following ministries and complete the final step of Network: Service.

The consultant and I agree the ministry to consider at this time would be:

M:

Ministry A _______________________________

Contact person _______________________________

Phone _______________________________

Ministry B _______________________________

Contact person _______________________________

Phone _______________________________

Ministry C _______________________________

Contact person _______________________________

Phone _______________________________

My Consultant was _______________________________

Phone _______________________ Date ____________

CONSULTANT FOLLOW-UP REPORT

NETWORK

Consultant: _______________________________________

Total Consulted: ___________________________________

Total Serving: _____________________________________

Name: _____________________ Work Phone (___) ___________ Home Phone (___) ___________

Not referred because:	Referred to:	Involvement:	Reason
	Options	Yes Obs No	Why?
❏ Attending another church			
❏ Satisfied in current ministry	A. _______________ ❏ ❏ ❏		_______________
❏ Waiting: 3-mo 6-mo 1-yr	B. _______________ ❏ ❏ ❏		_______________
❏ Needs another consultation	C _______________ ❏ ❏ ❏		_______________

Comments: ____

Name: _____________________ Work Phone (___) ___________ Home Phone (___) ___________

Not referred because:	Referred to:	Involvement:	Reason
	Options	Yes Obs No	Why?
❏ Attending another church			
❏ Satisfied in current ministry	A. _______________ ❏ ❏ ❏		_______________
❏ Waiting: 3-mo 6-mo 1-yr	B. _______________ ❏ ❏ ❏		_______________
❏ Needs another consultation	C _______________ ❏ ❏ ❏		_______________

Comments: ____

Name: _____________________ Work Phone (___) ___________ Home Phone (___) ___________

Not referred because:	Referred to:	Involvement:	Reason
	Options	Yes Obs No	Why?
❏ Attending another church			
❏ Satisfied in current ministry	A. _______________ ❏ ❏ ❏		_______________
❏ Waiting: 3-mo 6-mo 1-yr	B. _______________ ❏ ❏ ❏		_______________
❏ Needs another consultation	C _______________ ❏ ❏ ❏		_______________

Comments: ____

Name: _____________________ Work Phone (___) ___________ Home Phone (___) ___________

Not referred because:	Referred to:	Involvement:	Reason
	Options	Yes Obs No	Why?
❏ Attending another church			
❏ Satisfied in current ministry	A. _______________ ❏ ❏ ❏		_______________
❏ Waiting: 3-mo 6-mo 1-yr	B. _______________ ❏ ❏ ❏		_______________
❏ Needs another consultation	C _______________ ❏ ❏ ❏		_______________

Comments: ____

MASTER SCHEDULE

DATE: _______________________________________

Time	Consultant	Prospective Volunteer	Home/work phone
9:00 AM	___________	_________________	_____________
9:30 AM	___________	_________________	_____________
10:00 AM	___________	_________________	_____________
10:30 AM	___________	_________________	_____________
11:00 AM	___________	_________________	_____________
11:30 AM	___________	_________________	_____________
12:00 PM	___________	_________________	_____________
12:30 PM	___________	_________________	_____________
1:00 PM	___________	_________________	_____________
1:30 PM	___________	_________________	_____________
2:00 PM	___________	_________________	_____________
2:30 PM	___________	_________________	_____________
3:00 PM	___________	_________________	_____________
3:30 PM	___________	_________________	_____________
4:00 PM	___________	_________________	_____________
4:30 PM	___________	_________________	_____________
5:00 PM	___________	_________________	_____________
5:30 PM	___________	_________________	_____________
6:00 PM	___________	_________________	_____________
6:30 PM	___________	_________________	_____________
7:00 PM	___________	_________________	_____________
7:30 PM	___________	_________________	_____________
8:00 PM	___________	_________________	_____________
8:30 PM	___________	_________________	_____________
9:00 PM	___________	_________________	_____________

NOTE: Block out one hour segments for each consultation.

Consultant Training Outline

The suggested training plan for becoming a Network consultant is:

1. Attend the Network Seminar
2. Be consulted
3. Observe two consultations *
4. Study ministry position descriptions
5. Review your church's structure of ministry and statement of faith
6. Training Day (Consultant's Guide) — a minimum of five hours is required.
7. Observe two consultations *
8. Join a consulting team with leader
9. Submit hours you are available to consult
10. BEGIN consulting

   * People in the first group of consultants in your church's Network ministry will not have the opportunity to observe consultations.

To conduct the training day

- Coordinate a date, time, and place for the training day
- Send a note to your consultants:
    Thanking them for their participation
    Detailing specifics of time, date, and place
    Requesting that they complete the pre-class preparation in their Consultant's Guide. If they have not yet received a Consultant's Guide, be sure they receive one with the note.
- Follow-up with your consultants to confirm their attendance, and pre-class preparation
- Conduct the training day, using the Consultant's Guide as the outline for the training. The following is a guide to timing and sequence for the training day.

Consultant Training Outline, cont.

MinimumTime Required (minutes)	**Activity** (you will need to adjust the schedule to include breaks.)
15	Welcome the participants and use the "Warm-Up" Activity (Consultant's Guide Appendix).
70	Review the material in the Consultant's Guide includes a break
60	Watch the Consultant Training Videoand Discuss*

*You may want to stop the video at strategic points and discuss what was just seen.

10	Introduce the Consulting Practice Exercise (Consultant's Guide Appendix). Explain to the consultants the objectives of the exercise, and how to do it. Be sure that everyone understands the directions, and what they are supposed to do before you set them to doing it.

Ask the consultants to get together in pairs. If there is an odd number of students, pair yourself with one of the consultants.

Make sure the consultants know they have 45 minutes to complete each consultation and 15 minutes to organize and discuss how the person playing the consultant did.

60	Have the consultants start the exercise:

After 40 minutes, let them know they have 5 minutes left for the consultation.

After 45 minutes call time, and have them start the feedback and evaluation step.

After 55 minutes, let them know they have 5 minutes left to complete the exercise.

10	After 60 minutes, call time and allow everyone to take a 10 minute break.
60	Reconvene the session, have the pairs switch, and the person who was the consultant become the volunteer, and vice versa.
15	Call the participants back together.

Ask the group to share their insights on what they learned from the practice sessions.

Use any remaining time to answer questions about Network in general or the Network implementation at your church.

300 **Total Time (5 hours)**

Warm-Up Exercise

Welcome to Network's Consultant Training. To get started, team up with two other people,* and share the following information:

1. Your name
2. How long you have been attending this church?
3. Your
   - Passions?
   - Spiritual Gifts?
   - Personal Style?
4. What sparked your interest in Network?
5. Why have you decided to become a Network consultant?

* If you have a total of five or less people in this training session, stay together to do this exercise.

Consulting Practice

Objective

The objective of this exercise is to give you a chance to practice conducting a Network consulting session from start to finish.

Overview

This exercise is a "role-play." That is, you and a partner will each take a turn at the following roles:

1. Consultant In this role, you will play yourself as a Network consultant, meeting with a volunteer who has just completed the Network Discovery sessions.

2. Volunteer In this role, you will play yourself as a Network volunteer meeting with a Network consultant. Use your actual *Servant Profile* and *Personal Resources Survey* forms in the consulting process.

Directions

- This exercise will take approximately two hours. One hour for each of the practice consulting sessions, with a few minutes in-between for you to take a break.

- Start by deciding who will be the first to be the consultant, and "consultee."

- Conduct the consulting session following the steps in this Consultant's Guide.

- At the conclusion of the consulting session, complete the evaluation forms. If you were the consultant, complete the "Consulting Practice Self-Evaluation," if you were the volunteer complete the "Consulting Practice Feedback."

- After completing the forms, take a few minutes to talk about the consulting session. If you were the volunteer, provide the consultant with feedback on how he or she did. If you were the consultant, ask questions about any areas where you are unsure about how well you did, or how you came across to the volunteer.

- After taking a break, switch roles, and repeat the process.

Consulting Practice Feedback

Did the consultant:

❏ Set the mood (make you feel at home, break the ice, put you at ease)?

❏ Determine your motivation for serving?

❏ Help you interpret your *Servant Profile* and *Personal Resources Survey*?

❏ Help you assess your availability and spiritual maturity?

❏ Identify three possible ministries?

❏ Bring the consultation to a positive close, and confirm that you are clear on what you are supposed to do next?

What would you say you observed to be this person's three greatest strengths as a Network consultant?

1. ____

____

2. ____

____

3. ____

What recommendations for improvement as a Network consultant would you like to suggest to this person?

1. ____

____

2. ____

____

3. ____

Consulting Practice Self-evaluation

Evaluate yourself on the following. This is entirely for your own benefit, you will not be asked to turn in this form.

What would you say went particularly well in the consulting session you just conducted?

1. _______________________________________

____

2. _______________________________________

____

3. _______________________________________

What are some things you think you could do better or differently in the next consulting session you conduct?

1. _______________________________________

____

2. _______________________________________

____

3. _______________________________________

Willow Creek Resources® is a publishing partnership
between Zondervan Publishing House and the Willow Creek
Association®. Willow Creek Resources® includes drama sketches,
small group curricula, training material, videos, and many other
specialized ministry resources.

Willow Creek Association® is an international network of
churches ministering to the unchurched. Founded in 1992, the
Willow Creek Association® serves churches through conferences,
seminars, regional roundtables, consulting, and ministry resource
materials. The mission of the Association is to assist churches in
reestablishing the priority and practice of reaching lost people
for Christ through church ministries targeted to seekers.

For conference and seminar information please write to:

Willow Creek Association
P. O. Box 3188
Barrington, Illinois 60011-3188